An Everyday Adventure Series
by Moji Taiwo

Grandma & her Munchkins

Go to the Library

Illustrations by Cristiana Tercero

For my precious Munchkins: Ezra, Caxton, and Amos.
Spending time with you boys brings me vitality and endless joy.

Copyright © Moji Taiwo

All rights reserved. No part of this book may be reproduced by any mechanical, photographic, or electronic process or in the form of phonographic recording; nor may it be stored in a retrieval system, transmitted, or otherwise copied for public or private use without the prior written permission of the author at mojitaiwo1@gmail.com.
ISBN (paperback): 978-1-7782838-3-3 / ISBN (Ebook): 978-1-7751235-7-6 / ISBN (IngramSpark): 978-1-7751235-9-0

Moji Taiwo
www.mojitaiwo.com

We rode on the Ctrain to the city centre with Grandma. Grandma gave us money to buy tickets for the train.

Do you think they were

Were they going

Maybe they were going

going to school?

to work or the city hall?

to the library like us?

There were many stops along the way and so many tall houses and office buildings downtown.

We got off the train at City Hall station. Across the street, we saw a wading pool at Olympic Plaza.

Suddenly, Junior Munchkin said, "Look, there's a huge glass house!"

Grandma said the glass house is the new City Hall.

But we went into the old city hall instead.

There was a tour guide there.
He showed us around and told us that the building was made of sandstone bricks.

He also showed us old pictures, tables, chairs, fountain pens, telephones and something called a typewriter.

It looked so strange to us.
We didn't see any computers or cell phones.

Then we went next door to the public library.

The library was big and busy with many kids and grown-ups.

There are so many things to see and do at the library.

Grandma told us to because Grandma

choose one activity each
couldn't be everywhere.

Baby Munchkin chose a book with animals and funny stories to read with Grandma.

Senior Munchkin chose to learn how to build houses with Legos and wooden blocks.

And Junior Munchkin chose to learn new card and board games.

We took turns with each activity. It was very nice to share.

After we finished our activities, we went to see a display of Indigenous and African arts.

We also borrowed books to take home with us because we wanted to learn more about these cultures.

Do you go to the library?
What do you do when you go to the library?

www.ingramcontent.com/pod-product-compliance
Lightning Source LLC
Chambersburg PA
CBHW040023130526
44590CB00036B/76